CELPIP Vocabulary 2020 Edition: All
Complete Speaking and Writing Part

by CEP Publishing

CELPIP Vocabulary 2020 Edition: All Words You Should Know to Successfully Complete Speaking and Writing Parts of CELPIP Test

by CEP Publishing

© Copyright 2020 by CEP Publishing

collegeexampreparation@gmail.com

All rights reserved. No part of this book may be reproduced, stored in a retrieval system, or transmitted in any form or by any means, without the prior written permission of the author, except in the case of brief quotations embedded in critical articles or reviews.

Introduction

This book contains all the most important words that you need to know to successfully complete speaking and writing parts of CELPIP test.

This material is perfect for any serious candidate who does not wish to waste time researching and learning new vocabulary the traditional way. This book will make your learning more efficient with less of your own effort, which means more spare time to review other concepts.

We tried not to create just a regular dictionary with a bunch of words, but chose only the most necessary definitions. Knowing these words will definitely surprise your examiner, in a good way.

Accustomed

Familiar with something; usual (for example: She quickly became accustomed to new job).

Acquisition

Means the process of getting or obtaining something (for example: The children progressed in the acquisition of basic skills).

Adherence

Means the fact of someone behaving exactly according to rules, beliefs, etc. (for example: Strict adherence to the constitution).

Admission

Is a statement acknowledging the truth of something (for example: An admission of guilt).

Aggregate

Is a whole formed by combining several elements. To aggregate is to add together.

Akrasia

Is a state of mind in which someone acts against their better judgment through the "weakness of will."

Allusion

Is a figure of speech that makes a reference to a place, person, or event. This can be real or imaginary and may refer to anything, including fiction, folklore, historical events, or religious manuscripts (for example: When she lost her job, she acted like a Scrooge, and refused to buy anything that wasn't necessary).

Ambiguity

Means something unclear or confusing or it can be understood in more than one way (for example: There are some ambiguities in the legislation).

Amend

Means to make minor changes to the text (piece of legislation, etc.) in order to make it more fair or accurate, or to reflect changing circumstances.

Amicable

Means friendly, agreeable; characterized by or showing goodwill, peaceable.

Amusing

Entertaining and funny; causing laugh (for example: An amusing story).

Anxious

Feeling or showing worry, nervousness.

Appease

Make peace with; pacify or placate (someone) by acceding to their demands (for example: She claimed that the government had only changed the law in order to appease their critics).

Archetype

Means something that is considered to be a perfect or typical example of a particular kind of person or thing, because it has all their most important characteristics. For example, the United States is the archetype of a federal society.

Assiduous

Means persistent, hard-working. If you call someone assiduous, it means they're careful, methodical and very persistent.

Assume

To believe that something is true, even though you have no proof (for example: I'm assuming everyone here has a mobile phone).

Attrition

The process of gradually making something weaker and destroying it through sustained attack or pressure (for example: Terrorist groups and the government have been engaged in a costly war of attrition).

Augment

Make (something) greater by adding to it; to increase the size or value of something (for example: We need to augment the ring to five).

Austere

Means stern and forbidding. If you describe something as austere, you approve of its plain and simple appearance.

Avail

To be of use, help, worth, or advantage (to), as in accomplishing an end (for example: My attempts to improve the situation were of little/no avail).

Backlog

Means a number of things which have not yet been done but which need to be done (for example: I've got a huge backlog of work to do).

Banter

Good-humored, playful conversation; the playful and friendly exchange of teasing remarks.

Beforehand

At an earlier or preceding time; in advance; prior to; earlier (than a particular time).

Benevolent

Friendly and helpful; characterized by or expressing goodwill or kindly feelings.

Benign

Means pleasant, gentle, and kind (for example: A benign old lady).

Bewilder

To become perplexed and confused (for example: Beware of false people and situations that may bewilder you temporarily).

Bicker

To argue about things that are not important and trivial (for example: My parents bicker, but love each other).

Blare

Means to make a loud and unpleasant noise (for example: If something such as a siren or radio blares or if you blare it, it makes a loud, unpleasant noise).

Brackish

Means distasteful and unpleasant (for example: Brackish water is slightly salty and unpleasant).

Brazen

Obvious, without any attempt to be hidden. If you describe a person/behavior as brazen, you mean that they are very bold and don't care what other people think about them or their actions.

Brief

Something that lasts for only a short time or contains only a few words.

Cajole

Means to persuade someone to do something by encouraging them softly or being good to them.

Camaraderie

Brotherhood, partnership, jovial unity, sociability amongst friends.

Castigation

To criticize someone or something severely; verbal punishment. The word comes from the Latin castigus which means "to make pure".

Catharsis

Is the purging of the emotions, especially through certain kinds of art (as music or tragedy) that brings about spiritual renewal or release from tension.

Circuitous

Indirect, taking the longest route (for example: A circuitous journey/path is longer than it needs to be because it is not direct).

Coercion

Means the use of force to persuade someone to do something that they are unwilling to do.

Commensurate

Equal in significance; corresponding in size or degree.

Concede

Means to admit or accept that something is true after first denying or resisting it.

Conciliation

Is the act of placating and overcoming distrust and animosity; the action or process of ending a disagreement.

Confidant

Means someone to whom private matters are told. A confidant is the person you tell your secrets to.

Congruence

Is the consistency of different elements, objects, components of any structure, their harmonious work and consistency with each other, due to which harmonious work and integrity of the overall structure are achieved.

Connotation

Is a feeling or idea that is suggested by a particular word although it need not be a part of the word's meaning, or something suggested by an object or situation (for example, the word "lady" has connotations of refinement and excessive femininity that some women find offensive).

Construe

Make sense of; to understand the meaning, especially of other people's actions and statements, in a particular way.

Contention

The disagreement that results from opposing arguments; the act of competing as for profit or a prize.

Convergence

The state of separate elements joining or coming together (for example: If roads or paths converge, they move towards the same point where they join).

Countenance

Give sanction or support to; tolerate or approve (for example: If someone will not countenance something, they do not agree with it and will not allow it to happen).

Delectable

Delightful; delicious; extremely pleasing to the sense of taste.

Delighted

Means a feeling or showing great pleasure (for example: A delighted smile).

Delinquent

Means failing in duty, offending by neglect of duty. A delinquent person behaves in a way that is illegal or not acceptable to most people.

Denigrate

To speak damagingly of; to criticize something in a way that shows you think it has no value/ importance at all.

Deprivation

Is the lack (or feeling of lack) of material benefits considered to be basic necessities in a society; the lack of something considered to be a necessity in general (sleep deprivation, food deprivation, etc.; as an example, plants experiencing water deprivation will shrivel up and die).

Derogatory

Showing strong disapproval and not showing respect.

Deteriorate

Become progressively worse (for example: Relations between the companies had deteriorated sharply).

Deterrent

Means something immaterial that interferes with action or progress (for example: The stop sign on the corner is supposed to be a deterrent that discourages speeding).

Digression

The act of turning aside, straying from the main point, esp. in a speech or argument.

Diligent

Having or showing care and integrity in one's work or duties.

Disconsolate

Sad; cheerless; gloomy; hopeless or not expecting.

Discordant

Not in agreement or harmony.

Disparage

Express a negative opinion of (for example: He never missed an opportunity to disparage his competitors).

Dispassionate

Able to be rational and make fair judgments or decisions that are not influenced by personal feelings or emotions.

Docile

Easily handled or managed; submissive; ready to accept control or instruction.

Doctrine

(from Latin doctrina (meaning "teaching, instruction")) is a belief or set of beliefs, especially political or religious ones that are taught and accepted by a particular group.

Downshifting

Is the practice of simplifying one's lifestyle and becoming less materialistic; the act of leaving a well-paid but difficult and stressful job (escaping from "work and spend cycle") to do something that gives you more time and satisfaction, but less money.

Drudgery

Means boring and unpleasant work that you have to do.

Duplicity

Means dishonest behavior that is intended to trick someone.

Easygoing

Means relaxed and tolerant in attitude or manner; not easily upset or worried (for example: A friendly, easy-going type of guy).

Ebullient

Overflowing with fervor, enthusiasm, or excitement; high-spirited.

Elucidate

Means to explain something or make something clear.

Emancipation

Means any effort to procure economic and social rights, political rights or equality, often for a specifically disenfranchised group, or more generally, in the discussion of such matters.

Embassy

Means an official residence or offices of an ambassador (for example: The France embassy in Moscow).

Empirical

Means something that is based on investigation, observation, experimentation, or experience. If knowledge is empirical, it's based on observation rather than theory.

Enervate

Cause (someone or something) to feel drained of energy; weaken.

Enigma

Means a person or thing that is mysterious, puzzling, or difficult to understand.

Ennui

Is a feeling of being bored and having no interest in anything.

Enunciate

Means to pronounce words clearly so that they can be easily understood.

Epitome

Is the typical or highest example of a stated quality. If you say that a person or thing is the epitome of something, you are emphasizing that they are the best possible example of a particular type of person or thing (for example: This hotel was the epitome of British colonial elegance in Jamaica; Maureen was the epitome of sophistication).

Ephemeral

Means momentary, transient, fleeting; lasting for a very short time.

Equivocation

("calling two different things by the same name") is an informal fallacy resulting from the use of a particular word/expression in multiple senses throughout an argument leading to a false conclusion. For example:

"All jackasses have long ears."

"Carl is a jackass."

"Therefore, Carl has long ears."

Here, the equivocation is the metaphorical use of "jackass" to imply a simple-minded or obnoxious person instead of a male donkey.

Euphemism

(from Greek euphemia (meaning "the use of words of good omen")) is a polite word or expression that is used to refer to taboo topics (such as disability, sex, excretion, and death). For example, "passed away" is a euphemism for "died". It also may be a replacement of a name or a word that could reveal secret or holy and sacred names to the uninitiated.

Exemplify

Means to clarify by giving an illustration of.

Extemporize

Perform or speak without preparation.

Extrapolate

In general, it means using facts about the present or about one thing or group to make a guess about the future or about other things or groups. When you extrapolate, you use specific details to make a general conclusion. For example, if you travel to Canada and encounter only friendly, kind natives, you might extrapolate that all Canadians are friendly.

Fallacious

Containing or based on incorrect reasoning; not correct.

Fastidious

Giving careful attention to detail; very attentive.

Foible

Means a slight weakness in someone's character (for example: The minor foible in the woman's character made her unsuitable for the career she really wanted).

Forbidden

Not allowed, especially by law; banned (for example: Smoking is forbidden in the metro).

Frenzy

Is a state or period of uncontrolled excitement or wild behavior. Frenzy is often used when talking about a group of people (or animals) who get worked up at the same time about the same thing.

Frustration

Can be described as the feeling of being upset or annoyed as a result of being unable to change or achieve something. There are two types of frustration: internal and external. Internal frustration may arise from challenges in fulfilling personal goals, desires, instinctual drives and needs, or dealing with perceived deficiencies, such as a lack of confidence or fear of social situations. External causes of frustration involve conditions outside an individual's control.

Gangling

Unusually tall and thin; not able to move gracefully.

Gestalt

Something that has particular qualities when you consider it as a whole which is not obvious when you consider only the separate parts of it.

Grandiloquent

Style or way of using language in very complex way, in order to attract admiration and attention; big words used in a overly self-assured way.

Groggy

Feeling tired, weak, or confused, especially because you are ill or have not had enough sleep.

Gullible

Easily persuaded to believe something.

Hackneyed

Means something cliche that has been overused or done too much.

Hitherto

Means up to this point; until the present time.

Immersion

Means the fact of becoming completely involved in something (like project, subject, etc.).

Impetuous

Means rash, impulsive, acting without thinking.

Implications

Is the effect that decision or action will have on something in the future (for example: Our company is cutting back its spending and I wonder what the implications will be for my department).

Incensed

Angered at something unjust or wrong (for example: Teacher was incensed at his lack of concentration).

Inchoate

Not completely developed or clear. If something is inchoate, it is new or not yet properly developed.

Inconsequential

Unimportant, trivial (for example: His work seems trivial and inconsequential).

Indelible

Not able to be removed or erased. An example of indelible is ink that cannot be washed out of a shirt.

Indigenous

Indigenous people or things belong to the country in which they are found, rather than coming there from another country.

Indolent

Wanting to avoid activity or exertion; lazy, slothful.

Inexorable

Incapable of being persuaded or placated; continuing without any possibility of being stopped.

Inferior

Means lower in rank, status, or quality; not as good as someone or something else.

Ingrate

A person who shows no gratitude; ungrateful.

Insurgent

A rebel or revolutionary; in opposition to a civil authority or government.

Intervention

Is an orchestrated attempt by one or many people - usually family and friends - to get someone to seek professional help with an addiction or some kind of traumatic event or crisis, or other serious problem; when a group of friends gets together to help out another friend who has a problem, like drugs, manic depression, beating his wife, etc. usually involves an informal get-together during which the friends all sit down and talk with the person having problems.

Intransigent

Refusing to compromise, often on an extreme opinion (for example: The company is intransigent and rejects any notion of a settlement).

Intrepid

(from Latin intrepidus, formed from the prefix in (not) + trepidus (alarmed)) - extremely brave and showing no fear of dangerous situations; fearless; adventurous (often used for rhetorical or humorous effect).

Intrinsic

Essential; extremely important (for example: Access to the internet is intrinsic to a high quality of life).

Inveterate

Habitual; someone who does something very often.

Jaded

Bored or lacking enthusiasm, typically because you have experienced something too many times.

Jejune

Understanding or describing something in a way that is too simple, naive, or simplistic.

Jubilation

Is a feeling of great happiness, triumph or joy.

Leisure

Means a time when one is not working or occupied; free time.

Loquacious

Talking or tending to talk a great deal or freely; talkative; garrulous.

Ludicrous

So foolish, stupid, unreasonable, or inappropriate as to be amusing; ridiculous.

Lucid

Very clear and easy to understand.

Maddening

Means extremely annoying or displeasing.

Malicious

Unkind and showing a strong feeling of wanting to hurt someone (for example: Malicious rumours).

Mediocre

Not very good; of average quality and you think it should be better (for example: The acting in this film is mediocre).

Memorandum

Is a short written report prepared specially for a person or group of people that contains information about a particular matter.

Mercurial

Characterized by rapid change or temperament; sudden or unpredictable changes of mood or mind.

Metaphor

Is a figure of speech that directly refers to one thing by mentioning another for rhetorical effect. It does not use a word in its basic literal sense. Instead, it uses a word in a kind of comparison.

"I beat him with a stick" - literal meaning of "beat".

"I beat him in an argument" - metaphorical meaning of "beat".

Mettle

Means a person's ability to cope well with difficulties; strong-willed.

Misalliance

Means an unsuitable or unhappy alliance (especially with regard to marriage).

Modicum

A small quantity of a particular thing (for example: I was pleased with the overall response and I think we collectively felt a modicum of relief).

Mundane

Means ordinary, commonplace. Something that is mundane is very ordinary and not at all interesting or unusual. In subcultural and fictional uses, it is a person who does not belong to a particular group, according to the members of that group.

Nonchalant

Calm, casual, seeming unexcited; behaving in a calm manner, often in a way that suggests you are not interested or do not care.

Novice

A beginner, someone without training or experience.

Nugatory

Worth nothing or of little value/importance.

Obfuscation

Is the act or an instance of making something obscure, dark, or difficult to understand; the obscuring of the intended meaning of a communication by making the message difficult to understand, usually with confusing and ambiguous language.

Opaque

Not able to be seen through; not easily understood. Use the adjective opaque either for something that doesn't allow light to pass through (like a heavy curtain) or for something difficult to understand.

Ostensible

Stated or appearing to be true, but not necessarily so (for example: This new archaeological discovery is an ostensible source of hundreds of valuable artifacts).

Ostentation

Is a show of something such as money, power, or skill that is intended to impress people.

Outbreak

Is a sudden occurrence of something unwelcome, such as war or disease. This term most commonly used in epidemiology. When more cases of a disease than expected are recorded in one area an outbreak is declared.

Outlier

Means an extreme deviation from the mean; a person, thing, or fact that is so different that can't be used for general conclusions.

Oxymoron

Is a combination of two words used together that have, or seem to have, opposite meanings. Some examples of an oxymoron: Great Depression; cruel to be kind; painfully beautiful; alone together; wise fool; true myth, etc.

Paradigm

Is a model of something, or a very clear and typical example of something; a distinct set of concepts or thought patterns, including theories, research methods, postulates, and standards for what constitutes legitimate contributions to a field.

Parsimonious

Excessively unwilling to spend money or use resources.

Perfidious

Faithless, disloyal, untrustworthy. If you describe someone as perfidious, you mean that they have betrayed someone or cannot be trusted.

Perpetual

Continuing forever or indefinitely; never ending or changing.

Pert

Characterized by a lightly saucy or impudent quality.

Pile

Means a heap of things lying one on top of another (for example: She placed the books in a neat pile).

Plethora

Means a very large amount of something, especially a larger amount than you need, want, or can deal with.

Polemic

An aggressive argument against a specific opinion, doctrine, etc.

Postulate

Means something assumed without proof as being self-evident or generally accepted, especially when used as a basis for an argument; a fundamental element; a basic principle. Sometimes postulates are not obviously correct, but are required for their consequences.

Pragmatic

Dealing with the problems that exist in a reasonable and logical way instead of depending on theories.

Prattle

Means to talk in a silly way for a long time about things that are not important or without saying anything important.

Precipitate

Means to make something happen quickly, suddenly or sooner than expected.

Preponderance

Exceeding in heaviness; the largest part or greatest amount. If there's a preponderance of something, there is a lot of it.

Prevaricate

Means to avoid telling the truth by not directly answering a question.

Procrastination

Is the avoidance of doing a task that needs to be accomplished; the behavior of putting off actions or tasks to a later time. Sometimes, procrastination takes place until the "last minute" before a deadline. A procrastinator is a person who delays or puts things off (like work or other actions).

Proliferation

Is a rapid increase in the number or amount of something.

Prosaic

Dull, commonplace; without interest, imagination, and excitement.

Protract

Lengthen in time; cause to be or last longer. If you have a disagreement with a friend that you continue for days, you are protracting the argument.

Prudent

Careful, cautious; avoiding risks.

Queue

Is a line of people waiting for something (for example: Are you in the queue for tickets?).

Quintessence

Is the most typical example of something. For example, the Parthenon in Greece was considered the quintessence of the perfectly proportioned building.

Quixotic

Hopeful or romantic in a way that is extremely idealistic; unrealistic and impractical.

Rancorous

Means hateful. A rancorous argument or person is full of bitterness and anger.

Reclusive

Preferring to live in isolation; avoiding the company of other people.

Recondite

Means something that is difficult or impossible for most to understand, or that most people don't know about.

Refute

Prove to be wrong or false; overthrow by argument, evidence, or proof.

Rejuvenate

To make someone feel or look younger or have more energy (for example: Rejuvenating therapy).

Remiss

Means careless and not doing a duty well enough; lacking care or attention to duty (for example: He was extremely remiss in performing the tasks).

Renovation

Repair, making something new again.

Repudiate

Refuse to accept, acknowledge, ratify, or recognize as valid.

Rigid

Something that fixed; not flexible; not able to be bent or moved (for example: His face rigid with pain; I was rigid with fear; rigid exam schedule).

Rubicon

Is a point of no return; to cross/pass the Rubicon means to take a decisive, irrevocable step.

Sacrosanct

Holy, something that should not be criticized.

Salient

Significant; conspicuous; most important (for example: One of the salient differences between Amanda and John is that Amanda is a couple of kilos heavier; Only salient points can be indicated; The salient facts are the most important facts).

Schism

Division of a group into opposing factions. When there is a schism, a group or organization divides into two groups as a result of differences in thinking and beliefs.

Scrupulous

Characterized by extreme care and great effort; extremely attentive to details; very concerned to avoid doing wrong.

Scrutinize

To look at something very closely or very carefully.

Shatter

Means to break suddenly into very small pieces, or to make something break in this way.

Spurious

Means plausible but false; not being what it purports to be; fake.

Stagnation

(from Latin stagnatum (meaning "standing water, pond, and swamp")) is the state of lack of activity, growth, or development.

Status quo

Is a Latin phrase meaning the existing state of affairs, particularly with regard to social or political issues. In the sociological sense, it generally applies to maintain or change existing social structure and values.

Superficial

Appearing to be true or real only until examined more closely.

Supplicant

Is a person who asks someone who is in a position of power for something in a very humble way. If you pray every night to be accepted to your dream college, you can call yourself a supplicant.

Synecdoche

Is a figure of speech in which a part is made to represent the whole or vice versa. If you buy a car and you say to your friends that you just got a new set of wheels, you're using synecdoche - you're using the wheels, which are part of a car, to refer to the whole car ("a pair of hands" is a synecdoche for "a worker"; "the law" for "a police officer").

Synergy

Is the combined power of a group of things when they are working together that is greater than the total power achieved by each working separately.

Taboo

Is a vehement prohibition of an action based on the belief that such behavior is either too sacred or too accursed for ordinary individuals to undertake.

Taciturn

Means uncommunicative. Someone who is taciturn does not speak often and does not say very much.

Tatty

Old and in bad condition (for example: The stairs looked a bit tatty for a house which has been open only for a few days).

Tautology

Is the use of different words to say the same thing twice in the same statement. The word tautology is derived from the Greek word tauto (meaning "the same") and logos (meaning "a word or an idea"). For example, "They spoke in turn, one after the other" is considered a tautology because "in turn" and "one after the other" mean the same thing.

Teeming

Abundantly filled or swarming with something, as with people (for example: The Internet is teeming with viruses).

Tenacious

Determined to do something and unwilling to stop trying even when the situation becomes difficult, keeping a firm grip on.

Tortuous

Indirect; winding; with many turns and changes of direction.

Underlie

Be the cause or basis of something (for example: What really underlies most heart disease?).

Unkempt

Not properly maintained or cared for (for example: His hair was unkempt and dirty).

Verisimilitude

Being believable, or having the appearance of being true (for example: You can improve your game by using the real sounds of the ocean, to create verisimilitude).

Vicarious

Experienced as a result of watching, listening to, or reading about the activities of other people, rather than by doing the activities yourself. For example, lots of people use television as their vicarious form of social life.

Vilify

Spread negative information about something or someone.

Vindicate

To clear from blame or suspicion; to prove that what someone said or did was right or true, after other people thought it was wrong.

Vitriolic

Harsh, bitter, or malicious in tone. Vitriolic language or behaviour is cruel and full of hate.

Volatile

Likely to change rapidly and unpredictably (for example: A volatile person can suddenly become angry or violent).

Watershed

Literally means a region of land within which water flows down into a specified body; but also describes a critical point that marks a division or a change of course; a turning point.

Wry

Humorously sarcastic or mocking; showing that you think something is funny but not very pleasant, often by the expression on your face.

Zeugma

Is the use of a word to modify or govern two or more words usually in such a manner that it applies to each in a different sense or makes sense with only one (for example: She broke his car and his heart; He opened his mind and his wallet at the movies; He fished for compliments and for trout).

From authors:

We hope this book will be useful in your CELPIP preparation. In order to remember as many definitions as possible and take the maximum from this material, we recommend you:

1) Fully read this book at least 2-3 times;

2) Write down for yourself the definitions that you remember better and learn them first;

3) After that, learn 3-5 words a day, every day.

We wish you the best of luck, your CEP Publishing Team.

CPSIA information can be obtained
at www.ICGtesting.com
Printed in the USA
LVHW060838031020
667790LV00006BA/382